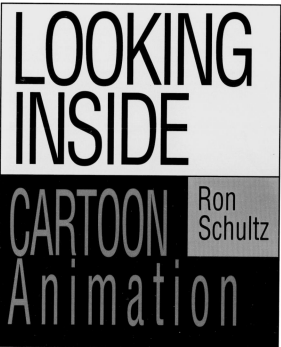

LOOKING INSIDE

CARTOON
Ron
Schultz

Animation

ILLUSTRATED BY
Chris Brigman

John Muir Publications
Santa Fe, New Mexico

ACKNOWLEDGMENTS

I would like to express my grateful appreciation to the following people for their willing cooperation, open phone lines, and excellent information. Without them, this book would not have been possible. From DIC Enterprises, Robby London, Andy Heyward, John Michaeli, Elisa Bruley, Lori Crawford, Stacey Gallishaw, Tony Collingwood, Teri Shikasho, Susan Odjakjian, Donald Zappala, Darrell McNeil, Michael Swanigan, Kassi Galinos, Melissa Gentry, Jill Goularte, and Joy Tashjian. In addition, I'd like to express my continued gratitude to the staff of John Muir Publications for their support, ideas, and a wonderful working environment.

This book is dedicated to
Johana & Emily
My two animation experts

John Muir Publications, P.O. Box 613, Santa Fe, NM 87504

First edition. First printing September 1992

Library of Congress Cataloging-in-Publication Data
Schultz, Ron (Ronald), 1951-
    Looking inside cartoon animation / Ron Schultz. — 1st ed.
      p. cm. — (X-ray vision)
    Includes index.
    Summary: Describes the process of cartoon animation, from script to final product.
    ISBN 1-56261-066-X (pbk.)
    1. Animated films—Juvenile literature.   [1. Animation (Cinematography)] I. Title. II. Series.
NC1765.S38   1992
741.5'8—dc20
                                   92-14122
                                     CIP
                                     AC

Design: Ken Wilson
Illustrations: Chris Brigman
Photographs: Rose Shoshana
Typeface: ITC Benguiat Gothic
Printer: Inland Press

Distributed to the book trade by
W. W. Norton & Co.
New York, New York

Distributed to the education market by
The Wright Group
19201 120th Avenue NE
Bothell, WA 98011

CONTENTS

INTRODUCTION

So, you want to look inside cartoon animation. Let Inspector Gadget be your guide. I know *everything* there is to know about it. After all, I am an animated cartoon character, not a real person. Yes, I know I seem so alive, but it takes lots of people doing lots of spectacular and creative things to allow me to stay hot on the trail of that dastardly Dr. Claw and his MAD minions. Yes, even the great Inspector Gadget sometimes needs help to come out victorious against the perpetrators of evil. There are writers, directors, storyboard artists, background artists, animators, sound technicians, animation checkers, camera operators, music composers, and sound, special effects, and dialogue editors, all hard at work to keep my gadgets in running order.

After the difficult assignments Chief Quimby has given me, uncovering the intricate secrets of cartoon animation should be a piece of cake for the old inspector. Being a detective, I'm an expert in finding things out! Discovering what cartoon animators do and how they do it should be a snap of the old Gadget fingers. Have no fear. Inspector Gadget is on the case.

Cartoon animation is the process of making drawn pictures move. The cartoon part is the drawn picture. The moving part is the animation. To animate means to bring to life, and living things move. That seems fairly logical, now, doesn't it. For instance, when I say, "Go, go Gadget," how do my legs turn into giant springs, sending me bounding over cars and buildings? How do animators make it appear that the Gadgetmobile transforms into all kinds of shapes as it zooms down the street? It's obviously time to proceed to the animation studio for further investigation. 👉

THE CARTOON

Hold it right there! Before we dash off to the studio, we're going to make a slight detour. First, we're going to understand *why* you laugh at me. Sure, saying funny things is part of it, but there's a lot more. Everything I do exaggerates or turns upside down some very basic scientific principles—principles that we take for granted but animators have to know a great deal about. These principles govern how the world works, how objects react in the normal world. Without knowing these things, an animator couldn't make things squish, tumble, fly, or move in a way that would be quite believable and at the same time make you laugh.

IT'S THE LAW!

Back in the 1680s, Sir Isaac Newton, one of the world's greatest scientists, proposed three laws of motion.

1. *A body that is still tends to remain still, and a body that is in motion tends to stay in motion.* This means that if a rock were sitting next to a river, it would stay right there unless something moved it. It also means that if a river were flowing, it would continue to flow unless something stopped it, like a giant dam constructed by that fiendish Dr. Claw.

2. *This stillness and movement can only be changed by an opposite force. The body will then move in a direct line from that opposite force until another force acts to change its direction.* This means that if I'm walking from the right to the left and a force moving from left to right collides with me, it sends me back from left to right. I remember just such a time in the jungles of India when I was headed west toward an ancient city to return a pair of tremendous rubies I had saved. To thwart me, Dr. Claw released a giant Bengal tiger that charged me from the east. Fortunately for me, my

gadget arms sprang into action, and I was able to turn around and head in the opposite direction away from that cat. That was, of course, until I encountered a tribe of outraged natives, who chased me to the south.

3. *Every action causes an equal reaction in the opposite direction.* This is one of the basic rules of animation, the one that will always get the biggest laughs. If you slam a gate open in one direction, that gate will always slam back in the opposite direction and catch someone when he least expects it. I know that's never happened to me, except for the time I went to that health spa and bounced on that trampoline. Every time I hit the trampoline, my force going down shot me right back up in the air the exact same amount.

Well, I think you can probably begin to see how an animator can use these basic laws to create some exaggerated and also very funny situations.

GETTING A LITTLE PERSPECTIVE

As we all know, when we draw pictures on a piece of paper, we are drawing on a flat, two-dimensional surface. The paper has length and width. Of course, in the real world, everything has three dimensions—length, width, and depth. To make two-dimensional things look like they have depth, artists and scientists developed an illusion called perspective.

The first rule of perspective is that the closer I am to you, the larger I appear, and the farther away I am, the smaller I appear. The second rule is that as two lines move into the distance, they appear to come together at a point on the horizon. You can experience this illusion by looking down some railroad tracks. The rails, which are like two lines, seem to gradually come together in the distance. They then tend to disappear at a point called the vanishing point.

In animation, this illusion is used in painting the backgrounds that appear behind the characters and action. Suppose I had to walk down a street. A line would be drawn across the page to show the horizon. Then the artist would draw the sides of the street so that they gradually get closer together, meeting at the horizon line. I would then walk between the sides of the street. With each step, my image would get smaller and smaller to fit within the picture the artist had drawn. In this way, it would actually look like I was moving away from you and toward the horizon.

THE PERSISTENCE OF VISION

Make no mistake about it, making drawings that don't move move is not only about art but about science, too. Animated cartoons appear to move because animators take advantage of "persistence of vision," a peculiar physical characteristic of the eye. To make things appear like they are moving at a normal speed, animated cartoons, like all motion pictures, are shown at the rate of 24 frames a second. That means each frame flashes only briefly on the screen—1/24th of a second, to be exact. When the image on the first frame hits the eye, it is picked up by the rods and cones. These are the sensory nerves that pick up light and color and are

attached to the retina of the eye. The retina sends information to the brain. Anyway, to get back to our story, before the rods and cones completely let go of the picture from the first frame, the image of the second frame activates them again. So, the eye holds onto the pictures it sees for a split second longer than they are actually on the screen.

You can experiment with this optical illusion yourself. Draw a large black dot on a piece of paper and stare at it. After a few seconds, look up at a white wall. You can still see the black dot, can't you? That's because the rods of the eye, those eye nerves that pick up black and white, are still holding onto the picture of the black dot. Pretty remarkable.

Another experiment you can try is to turn a light on and off rapidly in a completely dark room. After the light is off, even though you are in the dark, your eyes will still briefly see the light. Congratulations, you've just proven persistence of vision.

In both animation and motion pictures, persistence of vision is what allows the series of pictures, or frames, to blend into one another, so that they appear as if they are in continuous motion. This means when my head suddenly telescopes up from my collar, even though it may have taken 6 to 8 different drawings to animate that move, you, the viewers, see it as one smooth action. Let me tell you, the brain is an incredible part of the body.

So much for the science of animation. Now, finally, we can go to the animation studio so we can see how that science is used and animated cartoons are actually made. ☞

Perhaps I can't take all the credit for making animation what it is today, but in my humble way, I can safely say that I've made it clearer to my countless fans.

ANIMATION TIMING

Timing, one of the most important aspects of animation, is all based on the laws of cause and effect and Newton's laws of motion. Every action has a reaction, and each happens in a certain length of time that the animator must choose. How many drawings does it take for me, Inspector Gadget, to leap through the air from one spot to the next? If I were to make this leap in 6 drawings or frames, the leap would happen twice as fast as if I were to make it in 12.

Timing is also crucial in showing the weight of objects. Lifting a heavy object needs to take longer than lifting a light object; pulling a heavy bull will take more drawings than leading a dog on a leash.

Size is also a consideration in timing an animated sequence. A larger character needs to move more slowly than a smaller character to accentuate its size. Animators must also take into consideration the effects of friction and air resistance in timing sequences. If a character is walking against the wind, it will take more frames to get from one point to another than if the wind is *pushing* that character between those two points.

Timing is of the essence in showing special effects like water splashing, fire, or explosions. An explosion that takes 4 frames is much smaller than an explosion that takes 24 frames. The length of time needed to show the splash of an elephant diving into a pool is greater than the length of time to show the splash made by a mouse.

To make an animated cartoon really come to life, an animator must take all of these details of timing into consideration. Because without the proper timing, my falling on top of a couple of MAD agents and squashing them when they try to escape won't be as funny if it takes too long or happens too fast. As the great ones say, it's all a matter of timing, and, of course, mine is impeccable.

According to my trusty dog, Brain, a half-hour television cartoon show has between 16,000 and 20,000 drawings, or cels. My goodness, I didn't know that. I do know, however, that a cel is a piece of clear, flexible plastic, called celluloid, which is how the cel gets its name. It is onto this cel that an animation drawing is photocopied and then painted.

THE WRITER

But drawing pictures is only a small part of how animated cartoons are made. An animated cartoon actually begins with the work of a writer. These very clever people first have to make up the story. Then they write all the words the characters speak, called dialogue, and the majority of the action the animators and others will follow. The animation writer's tools include a typewriter or a computer, a copy of the show's "bible" (called a bible because it contains everything there is to know about a show, listing all the main characters and all their particular characteristics), and, of course, a very active imagination.

The writer often prepares a number of story concepts or storylines for the show on which he or she is working. These concepts are a few paragraphs long and tell the basic story. Sometimes, the story editor, the person in charge of the scripts being written for a show, already has a group of storylines prepared ahead of time. In this situation, the story editor simply assigns a story to a writer. However the story is chosen, the writer prepares a story outline that describes each major scene in the order it will happen. This way, a writer can make sure I catch the bad guys at the end of the show, rather than the beginning, where it wouldn't make much sense. Once the story editor and the producer (the person responsible for making sure the shows are made properly) decide they like the story, the writer begins writing the script.

TOON ANIMATION

Like all scripts, a good animated cartoon such as mine works because a writer tells a good story. A story requires a well-defined plot, the series of events that happen in the story; good timing, so that these events take place at just the right moment in the story to build excitement or anticipation or tell a really funny joke; and a strong structure, which is the foundation for the story that the plot hangs onto. Without solid structure, such as my constantly having to outwit Dr. Claw, the plot falls apart. And finally, a writer must also bring to life characters the audience cares about. Of course, these story elements are important for all stories, whether animated cartoons, movies, or books. But my writers are especially clever, which is why I'm loved by so many.

Television cartoon scripts are similar to television and movie scripts. Similar but different. In a TV or movie script, written for the incredibly limited abilities of real-life actors, a character's thinking and reasons for doing something, called the actor's motivation, are very important. Camera angles, such as close-ups of facial expressions, are also needed. And what the characters do is briefly described. In an animation script, motivation and close-ups of character expressions aren't as important: cartoon eyes don't communicate feelings like

Here's an animation time line that charts the history of cartoons from first step to *Beauty and the Beast.*

Early 1600s - Athanasius Kircher, a Jesuit priest, invents the "magic lantern," the world's first slide projector.

Late 1600s - Johannes Zahn gets Kircher's design moving by placing painted glass slides in a rotating disk. When spun, the pictures actually look like they are in motion.

By Tracy Thornell

human eyes do. Another difference is that an animation writer is expected to describe in great detail each and every camera angle and shot. For example, the camera sees my hand grow from my sleeve. My hat opens up, and my propeller emerges. I grab the bad guy. Dr. Claw's hand reaches for his monitor or pets Madcat. The writer has to describe everything the camera needs to record.

As we already know, animation writers exaggerate or completely ignore Newton's laws of motion. Characters can defy gravity and fly about at a writer's whim. They can also be squashed flat as a pancake and then suddenly rebound like an accordion. (It's a strange way to make a living, but I wouldn't trade it for all of Dr. Claw's gold.) Writers must be able to create all things imaginable and some things that are absolutely unimaginable. They create giant explosions, fantastic special effects, incredible locations and exotic settings, all without ever having to worry about the cost of such extravagance, as a live-action writer must.

I know it may seem like I've come up with these brilliant ideas on the spot, but before a single drawing has been drawn, a writer will have already described every move I make and every word I say.

INSPECTOR GADGET
#13 "AMUSEMENT PARK"

ACT ONE.

CHARACTER   DIALOGUE

GADGET   THE PERFECT DIVERSION...
               I GET TO VISIT A BRAND NEW AMUSEMENT PARK WITH
               MY FAVORITE NIECE.

               NO PROBLEM WITH MY GADGET MOBILE PENNY. IT'S
               ALWAYS ON DUTY.

               WHAT WOULD YOU LIKE TO D
               SIMPLE, PENNY.
               ONE PANDA BEAR COMING RI

               W MANY OF THOSE DUCK
               HREE, EH?   HIP IS MY
               LD WARN YOU THAT
               S.

THE STORYBOARD ARTIST

Once the writer has performed this creative magic and the story editor has approved the work, it's time to bring the script to life. I can almost feel the paint surging through my arms. But let's not get ahead of ourselves. The next step in making me into Inspector Gadget is to send the script to the storyboard artist.

The storyboard artist draws a rough picture of how each camera angle in every scene will look. A storyboard looks just like a series of Sunday cartoon comic strips. These drawings are made on large pieces of paper and are usually accompanied by a line of dialogue or a description of the action scene being shown. Storyboards show the complete sequence of a cartoon, how one scene follows the next.

Storyboards are drawn before the actual animation process begins. From the storyboards, it is possible to tell exactly what kinds of camera directions and pictures will be needed. By looking at these pictures in a drawn series, one after the other, one can see if there are too many wide shots or close-ups or not enough pictures of a certain character or if a story point is confusing.

By following the storyboard process, it is easy to tell, before any drawing is done, if the show is going to be interesting to watch. This is how I make sure all of my shows are as wonderful as they are.

Once the storyboard artist has completed all the different drawings for a particular show, the director and scene planners take over. They can then rearrange the storyboard panels to make sure the story's structure and plot move correctly from one point to the next. This is referred to as a cartoon's flow. They can also be certain that all my gadgets appear exactly when they are needed. By storyboarding, cartoon makers save a great deal of time and money, which is important because animation is a very long and expensive process.

Y ou can build your own zoetrope with a 4-inch-wide by 24-inch-long piece of cardboard or heavy construction paper. Laying the sheet length-wise, cut a series of 1/8-inch-thick vertical slices every inch across the cardboard. Tape the two 6-inch ends together to form a circle. On a separate piece of paper, 2 inches wide by 24 inches long, draw a series of pictures. For example, you could draw 12 pictures of a character raising and lowering its hand or a series of dots growing larger and smaller. Have fun experimenting with different patterns. When you've completed your drawings, place the circular cardboard piece with the slits on a record turntable. Then place the drawing sheet inside of the cardboard, with the drawings facing the center, and spin the turntable. Look at the spinning pictures through the slits on the side. Once you understand the principles of the zoetrope, you can redraw your pictures to perform all kinds of animated magic.

THE DIRECTOR

The director of an animation cartoon is very much like our own Chief Quimby. The director is the creative chief, the one who makes all decisions about the production of a show. The director looks at the storyboard and final draft of the script and approves the flow of the show and the look of the characters and the settings and makes sure everyone involved with making the show understands what is expected of them. This includes people like layout artists, background artists, animators, animation checkers, painters, and those in postproduction who will edit the show into its final form. I'll tell you all about them shortly.

As with live-action directors, animation directors often have their own particular, and peculiar, styles. One of the wackiest directors a cartoon character ever had to work with was the legendary Tex Avery. Avery had all his characters (and probably all his animators) moving at breakneck pace. Every reaction and every gesture were incredibly exaggerated. A cartoon dog's mouth would drop all the way to the floor, an excited character would bounce off the wall, or a character's eyes would pop and go halfway across the room before slamming back into his head. Then there's the great Chuck Jones, whose work with that gray bunny Bugs combined verbal jokes with knockdown action. How many times did Bugs cause something to explode in Yosemite Sam's face only to top the sight gag with a funny line? These are just a few examples of how a director might add a personal touch to the work of a writer.

But a director does more than just pass on his or her own style to a show. In many cases, directors were once animators themselves, so they know how to describe exactly what they want to their very creative animators. When they say a scene needs more *pow*, or less *wham-bang*, or a greater number of *whiz-splats*, the animators understand.

A TOON Time Line

1888 - Thomas Edison, of light bulb fame, invents a machine to record moving pictures to go along with his gadgets that recorded voices and sound.

1898 - The Lumiere brothers in France build the first motion picture projector.

Early 1900s - J. Stuart Blackton and Thomas Edison produce the first animated film, *The Humorous Phases of Funny Faces*.

1914 - Windsor McKay creates what many consider to be one of the greatest animation films ever made, *Gertie the Dinosaur*.

1919 - Otto Messmer transforms animation with his lifelike character, Felix the Cat.

13

As I explained earlier, the director must have a keen sense of animation timing so that when I fall from the top of a building, my gadget-copter blades appear to whisk me away before I hit the ground, or so that the time it takes me to sneak around a corner where my adversaries might be waiting builds suspense. They figure the different shots, making certain I've got the right amount of close-ups, long shots, medium shots, and profiles so that the cartoon will be interesting to watch.

The director must also make decisions about whether or not a particular scene adds something to the story. If it does not, the scene may need to be shortened or eliminated. This is part of the editing process. As we will see, editing is when all the different scenes of the film get put together in their correct sequence. To do this, directors work closely with the editors, who actually cut the long pieces of film and tape them back together in the right order. This is why the editing process is sometimes called cutting. If my shows weren't just the right length, they wouldn't fit into the TV time slot and the network and the advertisers would be very upset.

A TOON Time Line

1920s - Walt Disney, a Kansas City commercial artist, makes the first sound animation staring a dancing mouse named Steamboat Willie, later to be known to the world as Mickey Mouse.

1920s to present - Disney Studios develop and perfect nearly all animation techniques used today. So, even I, Inspector Gadget, owe a great deal to that tiny mouse.

1940 - Tex Avery introduces his outrageous, bouncing-off-the-wall-and-ceiling cartoons that feature a small gray bunny named Bugs.

TRACK RECORDING

Now, we come to the point in our story where my voice comes to life. While the storyboards are being drawn, the voice artists are put to work, recording all the dialogue or spoken parts of the script. Recording sound for cartoons is done on tape, just like you might use your tape recorder at home. Only this tape is much wider, because it can hold 24 different bands, or tracks, of sounds. As we will see, a lot of different sounds can go on 24 tracks. Two of those 24 tracks are used for all the dialogue my character friends and I speak.

Actually, track recording is another difference between live-action production, which uses real people, and animation. In the world of live action, the dialogue is normally recorded *with* the filming process. But ir animated cartoons, the dialogue is recorded before any film is shot so it can be used to time the action of the animation. The dialogue actually dictates how long a scene will be. All the sounds of each and every spoken word are broken down into tenths of seconds, so that an animator will know how many cels are needed to show me saying something clever, like "Wowsers!"

Either the director or the sound director will normally guide the voice actors through the script, directing their performances just like Steven Spielberg might direct Dustin Hoffman. Can you believe that in many cases, all the different voices in a cartoon show might be made by just two or three actors changing their voices? Would you believe my voice actually belongs to that wonderful comic actor Don Adams, who you have probably seen in his real-life form on the TV series, *Get Smart*. Sorry about that, Chief. I didn't mean to reveal that closely guarded secret.

In the world of cartoons, there have been some truly great voice artists who have performed dozens of different cartoon characters. The late Me Blanc was the voice of animation superstars Bugs Bunny, Daffy Duck, Barney Rubble, anc Sylvester the Cat. June Foray was the voice of Rocky the Flying Squirrel, Natasha Fatale, Broomhilda, and many others. In some cases, one actor may even play all the different voice in the same scene, switching back and forth between the different characters, asking and answering the same question. That's pretty amazing, if you ask me.

Ca-rrr-tooo-nn

THE TRACK READER

With my lines brilliantly delivered and the track recording completed, the recording is sent along to the track reader. This is probably the dreariest job in all of animation. It is also extremely important. In cartoon animation, animators can't draw characters speaking until they know how long it takes for a character to say a word. Then they can match the movement of the mouth to the spoken word. It's the track reader's job to listen to the completed recording and break down every sound in every word to the length of time it takes to say it. This time is measured in the number of frames of film it takes. You may remember that there are 24 frames or pictures needed for each second of a cartoon.

For example, say "Inspector Gadget." It might take two frames of film to say "In," three frames to say "spec," and one frame to say "tor." The track reader records this information on an exposure sheet, a frame-by-frame breakdown of every squeak, squawk, or squirm in the cartoon. By dividing these sounds and actions into single frames, the director knows exactly how many drawings are required to show the character speaking his lines or swinging from tree to tree fleeing from Dr. Claw's diabolical schemes. The track reading allows the director to synchronize the sound and action.

The track recording is run through a special counting and listening device. The track reader wears a pair of earphones to hear the length of each vowel and consonant spoken. This timing is recorded on the exposure sheet. It takes a track reader two days to break down, sound by sound, a half-hour cartoon.

Use a digital stopwatch and see how long it takes to say "Go, go Gadget." Actually, a track reader's device allows the track reader to replay the sound as slowly as needed to be able to distinguish a sound that might only last 1/24th of a second.

A TOON Time Line

1940s to 1950s - Enter stage left the likes of Woody Woodpecker, Tom and Jerry, Roadrunner, Wile E. Coyote, Yosemite Sam, Elmer Fudd, Porky Pig, and Daffy Duck. Also Disney makes full-length animation movies like *Snow White*, *Pinocchio*, and *Fantasia*.

THE LAYOUT ARTIST

As you are probably beginning to realize, lots of things need to happen at the same time to make a cartoon. In fact, while the track recording and reading are taking place, the approved storyboards are sent to the layout artists. Working with the director, the layout artist designs the locations and the costumes and stages the scenes, showing where each character will move. As I mentioned earlier, there are about 300 scenes in each half-hour show. A layout artist can usually complete 3 scenes a day.

When a cartoon series begins, before a single animation drawing is sketched, a layout artist has worked with the producers of the show to draw model sheets. These are very precisely drawn groups of pictures that show all the possible attitudes, expressions, and actions of a character. The precise drawing is necessary, because these drawings tell all the other artists who will work on the show exactly how to draw these expressions. This is important because there may be dozens of artists working on the same show at the same time, and all their work has to match exactly.

A TOON Time Line

1941 - Stephen Bosustow and a group of animators leave Disney Studios to start United Production of America, or UPA. Because UPA didn't have as much money as the larger studios, they completely changed the animation world by creating limited animation. They made their cartoons with fewer drawings, less movement, and more character poses. Sound and music became more important—as did characters like Mr. Magoo and Gerald McBoing Boing.

While the model sheets are being drawn, another layout artist produces a series of design sketches that set the tone for all the background designs for the show. For example, the backgrounds for my show will differ greatly from those in the *Ghostbusters* series or *Captain Planet*. All of these designs have to be approved by the director.

In addition, layout artists design all the disguises and costumes I wear on my various cases throughout the series. For example, once a cartoon series is being made and a scene is called for which takes place on a deserted tropical isle, a layout artist can refer to these model and design sheets for approved ideas and concepts.

Layout artists got their name because they are also responsible for deciding from which side of the screen I enter or exit during a given scene, at which point my neck stretches upward to get a better view of things, and where the action of the scene will take place. This is referred to as the layout of a scene.

It is also up to the layout artist to make a note of any moves the animation camera has to make while the cartoon is being filmed. Unlike live-action movie cameras that are actually moved around during filming, animation cameras stay pretty still. They can only make small moves. For example, the camera might zoom in from a medium shot to a close-up of my classic good looks, or move across a cel to suddenly reveal an evil MAD agent lurking behind a bush. The layout artist's notes are the guidelines for the animators who must bring these ideas to life.

ARM AND LEG GADGETS

HAND GADGETS

THE BACKGROUND ARTIST

Among the most beautiful and artistic aspects of cartoon animation are the backgrounds. A background is a painting on which a cel will be placed. It may be nothing more than a field of color, or it may be an elaborate environment. From a primeval forest of massive redwoods and low clinging ferns to the vast high-tech skyline of a modern city, backgrounds provide the texture for an animated cartoon.

Backgrounds are often painted in a slightly different style than the characters—and always in different colors. This is done so that the characters don't blend into the background and get lost. It is for this reason that backgrounds are often painted in watercolors, in deeper watercolors known as a gouache, or in tempera paints. These are all paints you may have at home. In fact, later, I will tell you how you can paint your own Inspector Gadget backgrounds and cels.

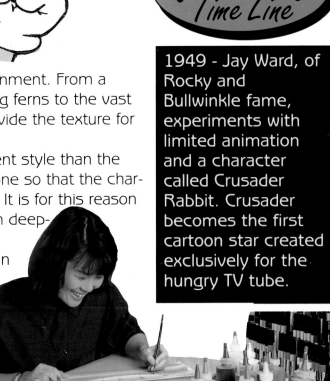

A TOON Time Line

1949 - Jay Ward, of Rocky and Bullwinkle fame, experiments with limited animation and a character called Crusader Rabbit. Crusader becomes the first cartoon star created exclusively for the hungry TV tube.

But backgrounds aren't always in the background. A background artist can create overlays by placing cels on top of a background. For example, a background artist puts a fire hydrant on an overlay so that when I walk down a city street it looks like I'm actually walking *behind* the fire hydrant. This gives the background the appearance of depth and lets me walk all around things rather than just in front of them.

THE ANIMATORS

With the background artists busily creating the settings, the director reviews the exposure sheets that are filled with the track reader's breakdown of sounds. Knowing exactly how long the dialogue scenes will be, the director uses the layout and storyboards to figure out how long the action sequences need to be to fill the cartoon's time slot. All this information is then brought to the animators.

Animators draw all the pictures that show movement. At this stage, these are usually very sketchy pencil drawings. It might take seven different drawings to show me walking across the screen. Each of those pictures will be just slightly different, as my legs rise and fall. If truth be told, the people who draw these pictures are the real actors in animation. They're the ones who have to bring all the characters to life, giving them their own particular characteristics—the way they move their eyes, hold their hands, walk, move their mouths, or react to things around them. It has been said that animators often behave as strangely as the characters they draw. More than one animator has been found trying out exaggerated facial expressions in a mirror or loping down a hallway trying to learn the movement of a particularly funny walk.

There are actually two kinds of animators. The first is called a key animator. This person does not draw all the pictures in the animated sequence, only the most important, most exaggerated, major moves. The key animator is also responsible for providing the creative expressions and touches that provide me with all my own special characteristics.

Using the model sheets and layout drawings from the layout artists as well as the exposure sheets, the key animator sketches out the basic sequence of the scene on sheets of paper very much like tracing paper. These animation sheets have special holes at the bottom and top so that they can be held on the pegs of an animation light table, which is a table that tilts up and down and has a hole cut in the center with a light underneath. A translucent plastic animation disk is placed over the hole to provide a hard surface on which the animator can draw. The disk allows light through so an animator can see the layers of pages of a sequence, one on top of the other. During this process, the animator

A TOON Time Line

1957-1970s - Joe Barbera and William Hanna develop a limited animation process that looked natural on television. Before kids can blink, the airwaves are jammed with Ruff and Ready, Huckleberry Hound, Yogi Bear and Boo Boo, Quick Draw McGraw, the Flintstones, the Jetsons, Scooby-Doo, and the Smurfs.

1983 - And before you know it, I, Inspector Gadget, enter the picture, solving cases people would never have guessed needed solving.

If an animator can draw between 20 and 70 drawings per day and there are usually 10 artists at work, about how many days would it take to complete just the animation portion of this process? Well, let's see. Go, go Gadget calculator. We'd figure the average number of drawings by first adding 70 and 20, which is, don't tell me, 90. We then divide 90 in half, and that gives us, that's easy, 45. So we can figure our animators can draw an average of 45 drawings a day. So, if 10 artists are drawing at the rate of 45 drawings per day and they need to complete about 18,000 drawings, how many days would that take?

ANSWER: 40

23

holds the different pages between his fingers, flipping back and forth between them to make sure the animation is smooth and flows properly throughout the movement. Each drawing is numbered, and the number of drawings that make up the entire sequence is noted. For example, if I stretch out my arms to snatch a bad guy, the sequence may require a total of 10 different drawings. A key animator might only draw numbers 1, 3, 6, and 10. When those drawings have been completed and it is determined how long the sequence is supposed to last, the animator sends the drawing over to the "in-betweener."

The in-betweener is the assistant animator, who is responsible for drawing all the pictures that go in between the drawings done by the key animator. In the sequence of my arm stretching out, the in-betweener would draw pictures 2, 4, 5, 7, 8, and 9. The in-betweener will then once again check the flow of the sequence by flipping through the pages. (You can get an idea of how this works by flipping the pictures drawn on the corners of the pages of this book.)

When the animators are finished, the drawings are cleaned up. This involves retracing the originals, eliminating the rough and jagged lines of the sketches, and smoothing them out. The result is a spanking clean line drawing. This process assures that I will always look my best—my coat properly pressed and my hat at just the right angle.

THE CHECKER

When all the animation drawings have been completed, they are sent to the animation checker. It is up to this person to make sure that each drawing has been completed correctly, that the animation is smooth, and that it produces the required action. The checker's tools are the exposure sheets, an animation table, and a disk. Holding the pages between her fingers, she repeatedly flips through the drawings. Any drawings that need to be changed are immediately sent back to the animators for correction.

After all the corrections have been done, the drawings are sent to be photocopied onto the sheets of clear celluloid plastic, called cels. Every drawing is photocopied, which produces a clean black-lined outline of the animated sketch. To get this black-lined drawing before the invention of copying machines, black ink was used. The animated drawings were hand inked onto cels using a pen or a fine brush. Those people who performed this process were called "inkers." Since the invention of the copying machine, inkers have gone the way of the dodo bird. Such are the ways of progress.

A TOOM Time Line

1991 - Disney Studios improve the process of combining computer animation and traditional hand-drawn animation to produce *Beauty and the Beast*.

25

THE PAINTERS

The black outlined cels are sent to the paint department, so the painters can apply the color. During this step, I get my fabulous complexion and natty gray coat.

Applying the acrylic paint is similar to a sophisticated paint-by-the-numbers operation. Each color used has a specific number. Model sheets, like those the animators use for characterization, are color coded and show exactly what color is used for every character and piece of clothing. Because everything is color coded, more than one painter can work on a show at a time. Over one hundred different colors of this acrylic paint, specially formulated to stick to the clear acetate, are kept on hand.

The painters turn the cels over and apply the paint on the backside. They do this to make sure that the layers of color are even and smooth. If the cels were painted on the front, all the color layers would make the cel appear bumpy and uneven. Painters also use a special technique in which the paint is spread rather than brushed on. This helps to eliminate brush strokes, which would ruin the illusion the animators work so hard to create. The painters push the paint right to the edge of the black outline, but in television animation they never go over it. Depending on the complexity of the action, painting one cel could take

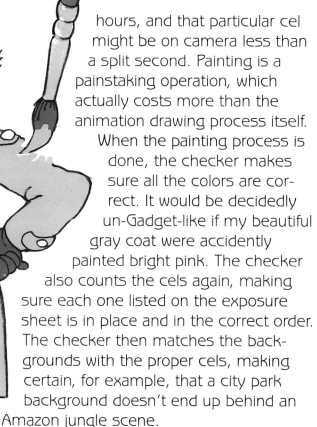

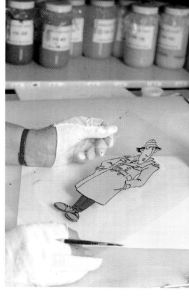

hours, and that particular cel might be on camera less than a split second. Painting is a painstaking operation, which actually costs more than the animation drawing process itself. When the painting process is done, the checker makes sure all the colors are correct. It would be decidedly un-Gadget-like if my beautiful gray coat were accidently painted bright pink. The checker also counts the cels again, making sure each one listed on the exposure sheet is in place and in the correct order. The checker then matches the backgrounds with the proper cels, making certain, for example, that a city park background doesn't end up behind an Amazon jungle scene.

Once the checker has made sure that all the cels needed are present, that all the colors are correct, and that all the backgrounds are matched with the right scenes, the whole package is sent on to the camera department.

THE CAMERA

Shooting the cels on camera is even more painstaking than painting them. The rooms are dark, and the pace is slow. No dust, or hairs, or lint can show up on the cels or they will be seen on screen. The film that animation cameras use comes on large continuous reels, hundreds of feet long. Each frame of film is shot one frame at a time.

The slightest misalignment of a cel on the camera animation stand could ruin an entire sequence. And remember, a camera person has to shoot 16,000 to 20,000 different cels. A minute's worth of screen time could take hours to shoot.

The animation stand itself is an amazing contraption. Looking something like a giant erector set construction, it is usually made out of steel, with a long crane arm on which the camera travels up and down. The camera can be tilted and moved easily so that if the script calls for a shot that moves in closely on my face, the camera operator can do so smoothly with the camera, rather than going through the added expense of drawing and painting an additional sequence.

The stability and precision of the animation stand is extremely important. Great precision is necessary because each cel has to be perfectly aligned, with the cel that came before it. If the cels don't line up in sequence exactly, I would jiggle and jump around the screen without having to use any of my gadgets. The cels are all punched with holes. And just like the animation table, the animation stand has pegs to hold the cels in place. These pegs are set into the stand's top. The top set of pegs holds the backgrounds and the bottom set, the cels. Laying on top of the cels once they are in place is the platen, which is a heavy sheet of hinged glass designed to make sure the cels don't move while they are being photographed.

Sometimes the script calls for the camera to move across a picture. This is called a pan. It shows an unbroken flow of movement from one place to another. To accomplish this, the pegs are attached to dials. When the dials are turned, the background scrolls by the camera. Suppose I'm on my way to the library and I need to walk from one city block to another. The camera operator slowly scooches the long background an intsy intsy bit in the opposite direction before each frame is photographed. The operator then repeats my walking cels (there's no point in drawing new cels if you don't have to) until I reach the library building drawn on the background. The background only moves a few hundredths of an inch at a time for each frame being shot. Any faster, and I would be flying rather than walking.

Many of the animation stands in today's animation studios are computerized. This allows the operator to program in all the camera moves, pans, tilts, and swerves, so that these precise movements take place automatically, are measured accurately, and look flawless. Computerized stands save operators a great deal of time and eliminate lots of errors. All the operator has to do is put the cel on the stand and take the picture. The stand and the computer do the rest. So, once again, the science of gadgetry makes the world safe for animation.

POSTPRODUCTION

Once the film has been shot, and I have, once more, solved the case, the film is shipped off to the lab for processing. The lab develops the negative, much like a photo store develops a roll of film. Because the negative must have absolutely no scratches or marks of any kind—there is, after all only one negative—they make a work print. This is what the editors will work with to edit, or cut, the film into its

proper length and sequence. I explained earlier that editing puts all the different scenes of a cartoon into the right order, which requires cutting up the continuous rolls of film that were shot into individual scenes.

Using a work print allows editors to make lots of changes—until the director says the cartoon is completed. Because it's a copy, editors don't have to worry about scratching it or writting on it.

Using the script and the exposure sheet, a preliminary edit, called a rough cut, is made. As the name implies, this is an unfinished, rough putting together of the different scenes. It's called a rough cut because it is just a rough approximation of what the final cut will be.

The *film* editing process in animation is minimal, because almost all the editing has already been done during the storyboard stage, before a single frame is shot. If a director has done his job well, if the timing and pacing of the show are correct, and the sequence of scenes has been set, the actual film editing process is fairly easy. In live action, this process can take months of cutting, viewing, and recutting, because the performances of real-life actors may differ from shot to shot, and because every scene is shot and covered from many different angles—unlike my performances, which are always shot right the first time. But then, I am a professional cartoon character, and I take my job seriously.

Once a rough cut work print has been assembled, the film editors go back in and snip off little pieces of scenes that run too long or add additional footage to scenes that need to be a little longer. This work is done on a gadget known as a moviola.

Sound Effects

After the work print has been cut to its proper length, it is sent to the sound lab so all the sound effects can be produced. At the same time, a copy is sent to a composer to create the music.

There are a number of different kinds of sound effects that can be created at the sound lab: those made with electrical gadgets that generate screeches, wind flaps, explosions, bells, bongs, and assorted weather sounds; and those created through a process called foley. Foley are live sounds. They're produced by people who re-create the sounds the cartoon characters make. If I'm walking on sand, or leaves, or gravel, or if I open or close a door, or pots and pans bang together, these people actually do these things in the studio so the sound matches what is happening in the cartoon. All of these effects are then placed on a recording tape that, as I mentioned earlier, has 24 different tracks, or recording bands.

While this is taking place, dialogue editors are busily at work at their moviolas. They watch the cartoon and edit the dialogue track (which was recorded way back when the cartoon first went into production) so it fits where it belongs on the film. The dialogue editor runs the sound track back and forth with the film to match the words as closely as possible with the character's opening and closing mouth.

Sweetening the Sound

When the dialogue has been matched to the film, it too is sent to the sound lab. Here, it is married with the sound effects, the foley, and the music. The sound is also "sweetened." This means sounds that are too soft are made louder, and sounds that are too loud are made softer. On a 24-track recording, tracks 1 through 4 are reserved for electronic information that indicates whether this is a monaural recording or a stereo recording. Monaural means the sound goes to one source; stereo means it goes to two or more. Monaural recordings take 2 tracks; stereo recordings take 4. Tracks 5 through 7 are for the dialogue, tracks 8 through 17 have all the sound effects, 18 through 20 are for foley effects, 21 and 22 are for music, 23 is blank, and 24 is held for the time code. A time code is a sound that is placed on both the sound tape and the film and continues from the beginning to the end of each so that the two can be matched up together.

A time code is put on every piece of film and sound tape used. It acts something like a stopwatch. The time code usually starts at the one-hour position. So both the beginning of the film reel and the beginning of the sound reel are marked at one hour. For example, if you wanted to go to Scene Two, it might be found on the film at the time code 1 hour, 4 minutes, 10 seconds, and 5 frames. The sound for Scene Two would be found on the sound reel at 1 hour, 4 minutes, 10 seconds, and 5 frames, too. The time code lets editors perfectly match the sound and the film.

Cutting the Negative

Usually, after a work print has been edited into its final form, it is sent to the negative cutters. Two or three people take the work print and the original negative of the film and cut the negative, using a special transparent tape to put it all together, so that it matches all the scenes on the work print. This is a very slow process: it takes about two days to cut a 30-minute show. But at this point in the process, the people at DIC Entertainment, who make my cartoons, do something

31

very special. With today's high-tech computers, DIC can perform this part of the process in a couple of hours, with just one operator. They have this remarkable new gadget. Wouldn't you know it. This is how it works.

Film today has a bar code mark on it, exactly like the universal price codes on packages you buy at a store. This mark, called a keykode, appears every 6 inches on the film. It is similar to the time code I described earlier. When the film negative first comes back from the lab, before any editing has been done, a copy of it is made on a special machine attached to a computer. The machine transfers the film onto one-inch videotape and using the keykode, marks where every different scene on the negative is located. This is called an edit decision list. Since television cartoons are rarely shot in sequence, the scenes on the negative are not in the order they will appear in the final product.

After all the editing has been done, and the work print is completed, it also is run through the same machine used for the negative, and all the locations of all the edited scenes are recorded. The negative is then put back on the machine, too, and the computer matches up the scenes on the negative with the scenes on the work print. For example, Scene One on the work print might be located at the 1 hour, 15 minute, 30 seconds, and 10 frame mark on the negative. The machine then goes to that point on the negative and copies that scene from the original to a one-inch videotape. It proceeds through the rest of the scenes, shuttling back and forth from the scenes on the work print and the negative, laying all the scenes down in exact order on the videotape. This final negative cut is then copied, sent to the television network, and broadcast to you.

As I said, DIC is just about the only major animation company cutting its negative in this fashion. But then, doesn't it make sense that the company that makes Inspector Gadget would have the most up-to-date gadgets? It certainly makes sense to me. ☞

GADGETS OF THE TRADE

There are a couple of very interesting contraptions and gadgets that are used primarily in feature film animation. One of these is the multiplane camera; the other is the rotoscope. Because a feature film takes so much longer to produce—a 30-minute television show is completed in 4 months, while an animated feature film can take 2 to 4 years to complete—these special tools are rarely, if ever, used in television animation.

The multiplane camera was developed by the people at the Disney Studios back in the 1930s. It is used primarily to give the illusion of depth. The multiplane camera is a massive, bulky camera stand with cel holders arranged at various heights up the stand, usually several inches apart. Backgrounds and foregrounds, painted on glass, are slipped into the holders at these various positions. Animators place the animation cels in between them, lighting the backgrounds, foregrounds, and animation cels separately. This creates a remarkable effect: everything looks more three-dimensional. If you've ever seen the opening forest sequence in Disney's *Bambi*, you've seen the multiplane camera working at its best.

The rotoscope has been used extensively by animation director Ralph Bakshi in his films, *Fire and Ice*, *Wizards*, *Fritz the Cat*, and others. The gadget was developed by Max Fleischer in 1917. It allows an animator to trace over live-action film, which gives the characters more lifelike motion and characteristics.

To use the rotoscope, an animator films a sequence with live actors, as in *Cinderella* when the Prince and Cinderella are dancing at the ball or in *Sleeping Beauty* when the Prince and Aurora dance in the forest. He then takes the filmed segment, places it on the rotoscope, and traces over on a cel each frame of the live-action sequence. These cels are then painted and combined with painted backgrounds, and no one ever knows that the movements are actually those of live actors.

ROTOSCOPE

OTHER ANIMA

Even though, as you might expect, I personally prefer cartoon animation, there are a number of other animation techniques that I should mention. They include photokinesis, made popular by those off-the-wall people of Monty Python's Flying Circus; puppet and object animation, brought to new levels of brilliance by George Lucas and his Star Wars films; clay animation, recently made famous by the California Raisins; and computer animation, which has been finding its way into live-action and animated feature films, commercials, and music videos.

PHOTOKINESIS

Let's first take a look at the two-dimensional animation of photokinesis. In this technique, animators use pieces of nonanimated artwork and make it move in ways it normally would not. For example, an animator might take a picture of da Vinci's Mona Lisa, frame and all, and have her hobble across the screen. Or an animator might simply cut out pictures from a magazine, paste them to cels, and move them around the screen. An animator might have a photograph of a snow-covered tree begin a conversation with a photograph of an ocean pier. An animator could use baseball cards to re-create an all-star baseball game by moving these nonanimated cards around a drawn ballfield.

This may seem like a fairly easy way to make animated films, but to do it properly, obtaining the effects and the look desired, takes a lot of patience and an excellent sense of how things can fit together. It also takes a certain technical skill with a camera and lights to really make these nonanimated figures come to life.

Photokinesis is also an excellent and relatively inexpensive technique for young animators to experiment with. Cut pictures from magazines, use photographs of paintings, or, for that matter, baseball cards, and shoot them one frame at a time with a movie camera, moving them slightly after each shot.

PUPPET AND OBJECT ANIMATION

Now, let's take a look at a three-dimensional technique. When the tauntauns and Imperial Walkers in *The Empire Strikes Back* slashed and crashed their way across those icy plains, you were watching puppet animation. When Sinbad the Sailor and Jason and the Argonauts, under the magical animated art of Ray Harryhausen, fought multiheaded beasts and swirling skeletons, you were watching puppet animation. When the Alka Seltzer character, little Speedy, tells you how effective Alka Seltzer is, that is puppet animation. When Godzilla attacks New York or King Kong climbs the Empire State Building yet again, that too comes from a frame-by-frame filming of these puppet beasties.

Puppet animation is a form of stop-motion animation. A movie camera capable of shooting single frames is used, and the puppets are moved slightly between each shot. As with all forms of animation, puppet animation works well only when the animator has a firm grasp of the science of animation—how and why things move the way they do—and is then able to bring that knowledge to the puppet. Who would have believed the rest of the action in *The Empire Strikes Back* if the tauntauns didn't appear absolutely real?

These puppets are made from all kinds of different materials, from sponge rubber to wood or plastic. These materials are formed around a wire skeleton of the character that has joints flexible enough to allow very small movements that can be held in place for a long time. Wires are often attached, as with marionettes, to move the various limbs of these characters and creatures.

In object animation, the objects are not recognizable characters. Remember the blocks flying around the room in Walt Disney's *Mary Poppins*, or the sand and shell counting sequence in *Sesame Street*? These are both forms of object animation. Object animators have shown oranges peeling all by themselves, without human hands. This style of animation is shot one frame at a time just like the other styles and uses invisible wires and strings to hold these seemingly magic effects in place. For each shot, the object is moved slightly, held in place and photographed. When all the shots are put together, you've got an orange peeling itself.

CLAY ANIMATION

In recent years, clay animation has reemerged as a popular animation form. Because clay is so easily molded and formed, it makes an excellent and inexpensive material for animation. Gumby was probably the first star of clay animation. But it wasn't until the mid-1970s that this technique developed into what is now known as claymation. As with puppet animation, in claymation, clay is placed over a wire skeletal body that can be moved in a lifelike manner. This technique won its makers, Will Vinton and Bob Gardiner, an Academy Award for animation in 1974, for a short called *Closed Mondays*. It was not too long after this that the California Raisins appeared on the scene and boogied their way to

---

ere is how you can use object animation to make your own animation film. Find a couple of pieces of fruit, some dolls, or some tools or other gadgets laying around your house. Take them outside where there is good light. Set up a movie camera that can shoot one frame at a time on a tripod to hold it still, and, shooting them frame by frame, put them into action. Remember, it takes 24 frames to produce just one second of screen time. You can figure out for yourself how many different movements and pictures it will take to film 60 seconds. The animation process requires patience, but the results are often remarkable.

fame. Although many advertisers and cartoon makers have been eager to use clay animation, there are only a few masters of the art. Vinton and Gardiner are the *grand* masters.

COMPUTER ANIMATION

One of the most remarkable changes in cartoon animation has come about through the development of the computer. Now, as everyone knows, I'm all for discovering new and useful gadgets to make life easier. And in some cases, the computer has really advanced the animation process. But at this point, in spite of incredible accomplishments, computers are still unable to do all the steps in the animation process. This is good news to all those animators out there scribbling away on their pads.

Computers shine when it comes to creating animated backgrounds. Unlike the flat, two dimensions of traditional animation, computers can work in three dimensions; in other words, objects have depth. Computer animation isn't very good for creating animated characters because it is still unable to make their movements appear smooth and natural. But for a background of a cartoon city with the camera flying around and through the buildings, traditional animation couldn't hold a gadgetbeam to it. Fortunately, computer animation and traditional animation are very complementary processes. They work well together.

Making a computer-animated cartoon is different from making a traditional cartoon. With traditional animation, most of the work is in making and painting all the animated drawings—16,000 to 20,000 of them. With computers, most of the work is in the beginning during the design

Clay is another good and inexpensive material for young animators to experiment with. Once a movie camera that can shoot single frames is set on a tripod to hold it steady, you can use various colored pieces of clay to construct a character. Then between each frame you shoot, the character can be molded slightly to change its action or position. As with all forms of stop-action animation, the greatest on-screen effects come from patience. Taking 12 frames to make a character lift a leg and start to walk will be more effective than trying to do it in 4 frames. Remember, for every second of screen time, you have to shoot 24 frames.

Photo by AutoDesk Animator Pro

Photo by Gene Bodio, TCA Inc. (AutoDesk 3D Studio)

phase—creating models and environments. The animation of these areas, as we will see, happens very quickly.

For example, let us suppose the producers of Inspector Gadget have decided that my show needs a new opening sequence. They want me flying my gadgetcopter through a teeming metropolis skyline and eventually zooming down on one of Dr. Claw's dastardly MAD agents robbing a bank. To accomplish this, the animator will have to combine computer-generated images with hand-drawn figures.

Combining Animation Techniques

In recent years, there has been a great deal of research in combining two-dimensional cartoon characters and three-dimensional computer-generated backgrounds. Disney Studios has again led the way. One of the most dramatic uses was the opening sequence of *The Rescuers Down Under* in which an eagle flies through the dry Australian terrain. Disney improved on its technique in *Beauty and the Beast* in that beautiful ballroom scene. The ballroom was completely generated by a computer, but the waltzing characters were drawn in the traditional way.

They were later blended by scanning the hand-drawn figures into the computer and placing them against the computer background. Both images were then transferred to videotape.

Getting back to my new opening sequence. The computer animator, working closely with the director and a storyboard describing every move and camera angle that will be needed, chooses a series of building block shapes to create the city skyline. By moving his computer mouse around the screen, the animator picks the different shapes and assembles the buildings in order. The director usually spends a lot of time making sure the animator is creating just the right look.

The animator uses a series of shapes—squares, spheres, cylinders, cubes—to build each piece of the picture. After the director has approved the basic wire-frame look of the skyline, it is time to apply the color. In computer animation, this is called texture mapping. Unlike traditional animation, computers can reproduce real world textures like glass or chrome on its creations. If I need to land on a giant chrome ball floating in space, a computer animator will create the sphere, then tell the computer to make it chrome. Instantly, the ball will shine and reflect the world around it. The animator assigns textures to each and every object in the picture. All this information is stored on a computer disk.

After the models have been completed and textured, it's time to give the computer the commands to animate them. Now, the buildings themselves might not be moving, but the director wants it to look as if I am flying by and through them, and he wants the audience to see things from my point of view—as if my eyes were actually the camera. The animator establishes a starting point on the background and a camera position, telling the computer this is point 0. The camera is then moved to where it will be at position 100, farther into the background. The animator tells the computer, "This is position 100, now create all the movements that take place between position 0 and position 100." And with a zip, the computer generates all the in-between movements between position 0 and 100. The camera is then moved to position 200, and zip, the in-betweening is computer generated.

The Final Test

After the entire sequence has been generated, a quick test is performed to make sure the animation is smooth and every desired angle and move has been made and recorded. Then the director gives final approval. If something isn't quite right when I swoop by an open window and a dog barks, the animator can easily make a few minor adjusts with the computer, and the sequence is saved. When everyone is happy, the animator gives the computer the instructions to create all the finished frames. The computer is hooked up to a special videotape deck, which advances the videotape one frame at a time. It might take several days for the computer to do this. When it has completed its job, my new opening sequence is added to the front of my show in the postproduction process. The great Inspector Gadget has entered the computer age.

Now that you thoroughly understand the animation process, because I have explained it so magnificently, I can once again put on my Inspector's hat and resume my duties as Inspector Gadget. Duty calls. Inspector Gadget is always on the job.

AFTERWORD

So, that's the story of cartoon animation. It's pretty amazing if you ask me. And what's equally amazing is that animation is experiencing one of the most popular periods in its history. More animation, for both television and feature films, is being produced today than at any other time. But it is important to remember that animation is not just about drawing pictures. I didn't become the great Inspector Gadget by accident. It took a lot of know-how and hard work. Believe me, to run computers and make all the calculations necessary to assure proper timing takes lots of education. To draw pictures that incorporate laws of science takes lots of study. Cartoon animation may seem like child's play, but to do it properly and artistically takes a talented, knowledgeable, and educated person. Just as I spent long hours honing my skills as a detective, it takes dedication to perfect all the necessary details of this amazing moving picture art form. Go, go animation!

DIC 1983©

X-ray Vision Series

Each title in the series is 8½" × 11", 48 pages, $9.95, paperback, with four-color photographs and illustrations and written by Ron Schultz.

Looking Inside the Brain

Looking Inside Cartoon Animation

Looking Inside Sports Aerodynamics

Looking Inside Sunken Treasure

Looking Inside Telescopes and the Night Sky

Masters of Motion Series

Each title in the series is 10¼" × 9", 48 pages, $9.95, paperback, with four-color photographs and illustrations.

How to Drive an Indy Race Car
David Rubel

How to Fly a 747
Tim Paulson

How to Fly the Space Shuttle
Russell Shorto
(avail. 12/92)

The Extremely Weird Series

All of the titles in the Extremely Weird Series are written by Sarah Lovett, are 8½" × 11", 48 pages, and $9.95 paperbacks.

Extremely Weird Bats

Extremely Weird Birds

Extremely Weird Endangered Species

Extremely Weird Fishes

Extremely Weird Frogs

Extremely Weird Insects

Extremely Weird Primates

Extremely Weird Reptiles

Extremely Weird Sea Creatures

Extremely Weird Spiders

Other Titles of Interest

Habitats
Where the Wild Things Live
Randi Hacker and Jackie Kaufman
8½" × 11", 48 pages, color illustrations
$9.95 paper

The Indian Way
Learning to Communicate with Mother Earth
Gary McLain
Paintings by Gary McLain
Illustrations by Michael Taylor
7" × 9", 114 pages, two-color illustrations
$9.95 paper

Kids Explore America's Hispanic Heritage
Westridge Young Writers Workshop
7" × 9", 112 pages, illustrations
$7.95 paper

Rads, Ergs, and Cheeseburgers
The Kids' Guide to Energy and the Environment
Bill Yanda
Illustrated by Michael Taylor
7" × 9", 108 pages, two-color illustrations
$12.95 paper

The Kids' Environment Book
What's Awry and Why
Anne Pedersen
Illustrated by Sally Blakemore
7" × 9", 192 pages, two-color illustrations
$13.95 paper
For Ages 10 and Up

The Quill Hedgehog Adventures Series

Green fiction for young readers. Each title in the series is written by John Waddington-Feather and illustrated by Doreen Edmond.

Quill's Adventures in the Great Beyond
Book One
5½" × 8½", 96 pages, $5.95 paper

Quill's Adventures in Wasteland
Book Two
5½" × 8½", 132 pages, $5.95 paper

Quill's Adventures in Grozzieland
Book Three
5½" × 8½", 132 pages, $5.95 paper

The Kidding Around Travel Series

All of the titles listed below are 64 pages and $9.95 except for *Kidding Around the National Parks of the Southwest* and *Kidding Around Spain*, which are 108 pages and $12.95.

Kidding Around Atlanta

Kidding Around Boston

Kidding Around Chicago

Kidding Around the Hawaiian Islands

Kidding Around London

Kidding Around Los Angeles

Kidding Around the National Parks of the Southwest

Kidding Around New York City

Kidding Around Paris

Kidding Around Philadelphia

Kidding Around San Diego

Kidding Around San Francisco

Kidding Around Santa Fe

Kidding Around Seattle

Kidding Around Spain

Kidding Around Washington, D.C.

ORDERING INFORMATION Your books will be sent to you via UPS (for U.S. destinations). UPS will not deliver to a P.O. Box; please give us a street address. Include $3.75 for the first item ordered and $.50 for each additional item to cover shipping and handling costs. For airmail within the U.S., enclose $4.00. All foreign orders will be shipped surface rate; please enclose $3.00 for the first item and $1.00 for each additional item. Please inquire about foreign airmail rates.

METHOD OF PAYMENT Your order may be paid by check, money order, or credit card. We cannot be responsible for cash sent through the mail. All payments must be made in U.S. dollars drawn on a U.S. bank. Canadian postal money orders in U.S. dollars are acceptable. For VISA, MasterCard, or American Express orders, include your card number, expiration date, and your signature, or call (800) 888-7504. Books ordered on American Express cards can be shipped only to the billing address of the cardholder. Sorry, no C.O.D.'s. Residents of sunny New Mexico, add 5.875% tax to the total.

Address all orders and inquiries to: **John Muir Publications**, P.O. Box 613, Santa Fe, NM 87504, (505) 982-4078, (800) 888-7504.